Stop the vacuum!
I want to get off.

How to involve men
and other family members
in the fun-filled joys of housekeeping.

by Toni Pighetti

TAM Associates, Ltd.
Oak Park, Illinois

Copyright © 1987 by Toni Pighetti

Published by TAM Associates, Ltd.
P.O. Box 285
Oak Park, Illinois 60303
(312) 848-6760

Printed and bound in the United States of America

Library of Congress Catalog Card Number: 86-50712

ISBN 0-913005-06-1

Cover Design by Michelle LeMoine
Illustrations by Scott Kiefer

Special thanks to Tommie Sue Arnold of Corpus Christi, Texas, who first exclaimed "Stop the vacuum cleaner! I want to get off."

More special thanks to Marion Newport Biagi, Jim Seidelmann, Barb Gearen, Mike Gearen, Marilyn Ricci, Ruth Prescott, Rosalind Larsen, Catherine Deam, Denny Webster, and Carlotta Madonia for their editing assistance, input, support or encouragement.

Extra special thanks to my family.

Dedication

To the young woman in Hampton, Virginia whose husband flat out refused to lift one finger doing "women's work".

To the woman in Oak Brook, Illinois, whose husband makes so much money that he refuses to take his dinner plate to the sink.

To the new mother who gave up her career and was told by her husband that she now had the entire housekeeping, child care and meal-related tasks as her responsibility while he got to fix the car and mow the lawn.

To the men I've met who are as much at home changing a diaper and doing laundry as they are at painting the house and paneling the basement.

Other publications by TAM Associates, Ltd.

THE NITTY GRITTY BARE BONES METHOD OF HOUSEKEEPING CALENDAR

THE CHILDREN'S ORGANIZER

Table of Contents

Introduction

Guess Who's on the Vacuum?

In AMERICAN COUPLES, Dr. Philip Blumstein and Dr. Pepper Schwartz observe: "Working wives do less house work than homemakers, but they still do the vast bulk of what needs to be done. Husbands of women who work help out more than husbands of home makers, but their contribution is not impressive. Even if a husband is unemployed, he does much less housework than a wife who puts in a 40 hour week."

Note: How clean should a home be? Each family has to make its own decisions based upon how much time members are willing to spend removing the dirt! If their priority is everything spotless most of the time, then they will take the time to accomplish this feat. Those of us who want to spend as little time as possible in cleaning must set our own limits as to what dirt is "allowed" and how much we can tolerate.

Dirt (in its various guises) provides a welcome home to bacteria, and encourages safety hazards such as grease fires in the kitchen. It damages our belongings (such as causing carpets to become threadbare before their time), and is generally unpleasant and unsightly. Remember, your home is the backdrop of your life. Unless it is your main reason for living, maintain it only enough to prevent frustration. Set your goal as *low* as you can!

Introduction

Guess Who's on the Vacuum?

You know who it is. It's a woman. She is stuck with the housekeeping responsibilities. It doesn't matter how much time she has available, it doesn't matter if she has a job outside the home or not, it doesn't matter if she has no children or if she has six children. And when the man of the house does do the dishes, he is usually "pitching" in, i.e., he's doing her a favor.

It's time we made some changes. Just because we thought we *could* do it, or because we thought we *should* do it, or because we said we *would* do it, doesn't mean we have to *keep* doing it.

But making changes is uncomfortable; it is especially difficult when it involves changing more than one person, but it *is* possible.

Consider the following questions:

Are all or most of the housekeeping tasks your responsibility?

Do you want responsibility for all these tasks?

Do all your family members share housekeeping responsibilities?

Does one or more member believe that they work hard enough outside the home and therefore should

9

be exempt from housekeeping tasks?

Do you agree to this exemption?

Have you ever compared the amount of leisure time that different family members take?

Why *won't* your children or spouse do housekeeping tasks?

Do they repeatedly refuse, insisting that it is not their job?

Do your children ask, "Why do *I* have to do this? Why can't *you* do it?"

When you recruit their participation, do they nod their heads in agreement with you, make an initial effort to help and then quickly revert to old non-working behaviors?

Do you feel guilty when they do help, but resent them when they don't?

Have you ever shared your feelings about housekeeping issues with your family?

Do you know what housekeeping tasks you'd like them to take responsibility for?

Do you know what your family's capabilities are?

Are you willing to give up control?

What *is* the problem?

Whose problem is it?

If the problem is that you want other family members to share in the housekeeping tasks and they are not doing so, then you've got the right book. And you've also got the problem. The other family members do not have this problem. They are happy with the current situation.

You might be angry because you are stuck with all the housekeeping tasks. Anger will not solve the problem. In fact, anger will only make difficulties greater. Please do not use this book to support your anger! Use this book to find a way to a solution; use it to achieve the goal of total family participation in housekeeping tasks.

Now is the time to evaluate your situation. Which family members perform housekeeping tasks? What do they do and how frequently do they do it? How much family participation is desirable and is it possible?

This is not a "how-to-clean" book. The issues I am addressing concern *who* does the cleaning, *why* this person does it and *how* the workload may be redistributed.

My personal experiences are referred to throughout the book. Not everyone will relate to all the details, but many women will empathize with my thoughts and feelings while struggling with these housekeeping issues. My story also provides a setting — the scenery — for discussion.

I hope that this book will give you:

- Knowledge that changing housekeeping responsibilities is possible. It is *your choice.*

- Techniques for making this change actually happen.

- Courage to begin and consistently work towards this goal of total family participation.

Somebody once told me that self-help books only helped the author. Setting aside the fact that I am such an author, I had to disagree with this person because I have personally been helped by several books. Because of these books, I made changes in my life. Although the books were the catalyst, *I* am the one who made the change. Reading the book may be entertaining, inspiring or motivational. To make a difference in your life, however, you must take action.

In *A Road Less Traveled,* Dr. M. Scott Peck encourages us to face our problems. He writes, "Problems do not go away. They must be worked through or else they remain, forever a barrier to the growth and development of the spirit."

You have the ability and power within yourself to change your life. The first step is to take the responsibility for your problems and begin working on solutions. You can do it!

In the following chapters, you will learn that family participation is not only possible, you will learn that it will actually benefit the entire family. Here's a brief description of each chapter:

Chapter 1, "So What's the Problem?" describes what is inherently wrong with the typical American division of labor in the home.

Chapter 2, "So What's *My* Problem?" continues to describe this problem focusing on my personal experiences.

Chapter 3, "Why are Women Chained to the Vacuum Cleaner Anyway?" examines the subtle reasons why women continue to take responsibility for most of the housekeeping tasks.

Chapter 4, "I'm Getting off the Vacuum!" tells the story of how I began to get the family to accept more responsibility.

Chapter 5, "Give Up the Guilt" recognizes that giving up guilt is much easier to imagine than it is to do. Guilt is destructive when it dictates our actions. Being aware of guilt, where it comes from and what it does to us helps us overcome this negative feeling.

Chapter 6, "Equalizing the Workload!" discusses the problem in terms of finding a solution and presents a plan for increasing other people's participation.

Chapter 7, "Sharing Housekeeping Tasks: How Other Families Operate." contains descriptions of various family situations. Other people's solutions may work for you.

Chapter 8, "Hooray for Jobs Outside the Home!" questions the myth that jobs outside the home are more demanding than the job in the home. It takes a logical look at the advantages and disadvantages of the two work place situations.

Chapter 9, "Housekeeping Tasks" This last section contains task worksheets. The tasks themselves are the nitty-gritty facts of housekeeping. Seeing them in print allows you to evaluate them according to your own personal requirements and standards.

Chapter 1
So, What's the Problem?

Don Aslett, WHO SAYS IT'S A WOMEN'S JOB TO CLEAN? page 17:

"a recent survey conducted by the American Family Physician reported that employed wives spend 26 hours a week on housework; their husbands spend 36 minutes a week."

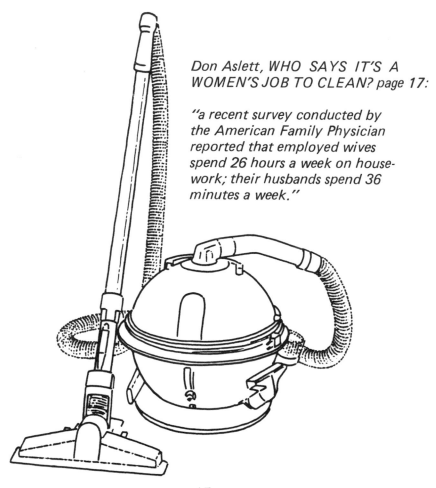

15

to more equal task distribution is women's own perceptions of what they should or must do to be a good wife and mother. They are still trying to fulfill standards set up in a generation where it was possible to do those things because a woman's full-time role was homemaker."

Because this subject concerns the behavior of many people, it is not just a matter of women getting over their need to prove their femininity by doing it all. There must then be a change in men's attitudes and resistance.

Which brings us to yet another problem!

Since men have not been expected to perform household tasks in the past, they will not voluntarily take them over.

And why should they! The messages our society continues to give them exempts them from most household chores. To confuse the issue more, the tasks that men do accept are not as menial as women's work.

You guessed it! A problem:

Traditional women's tasks are more repetitive, demeaning and less creative than the chores that men choose.

If family members are to share in the tasks, exactly what are they going to do? It is not only that women have too much to do. A major consideration is the division of labor. What is being done by whom?

Women's work usually consists of the dirty, messy, repetitive tasks. The traditional tasks that men take on are usually the occasional repairing, building or rehabbing, non-repetitive jobs — the kind that a three year old can't destroy 10 minutes after completion.

For example, men get to mow the lawn, panel the basements, repair the appliances, and some even take out the garbage.

Now, mowing the lawn takes time. It can be a very uncomfortable and strenuous activity depending upon the weather and the equipment. However, it only needs doing at the most once a week, and not 52 weeks a year. Additionally, the family can't undo this work ten minutes after it is done (OK kids, lets all go outside and tape the grass back on!). And once the garbage is put out, it stays there.

After a recent seminar, a woman told me that right after her first child was born, her husband said, "Now, I go to work and make the money. I'll mow the lawn and maintain the car. You take care of the child, do the cooking and the housekeeping." These few simple sentences sound as though the division of labor is equal.

That brings us to yet another problem:

It is easy to assume that a person who is home during the day has a lot of time for leisure.

This is especially easy to assume if you've never had to stay home and be responsible for all the household chores, all the shopping for family food and goods, all meal preparation, all day-to-day maintenance, etc., etc., *and* care for one or more children!

When my children were small, I had a lot of time to play tennis. The house was totally disorganized. I only did what I had to do to keep us functioning at a basic level. I couldn't complain about the unfairness of my situation because I gave recreation a top priority.

However, when I learned how to be "super-woman", I realized that for me there weren't enough hours in the day. Maintaining a home to the American standard of everything clean and in its proper place takes more time than a full-time job. It is a never-ending, repetitive, lonely activity for which there is no salary (merely room and board) and too little respect.

What is interesting to me is that when my home was always in terrible clutter, nobody could clean. On rare occasions I'd hire a cleaning person, but it took me days to prepare the rooms so that the dirt could be removed! Later, when I was controlling the clutter, it was possible to establish cleaning routines.

However, I did not make the dirt. Yet here I was with all the dirt-removal responsibilities. Eliminating grease in the kitchen, dust on the lamps, stains in the toilet and lint on the rugs became a constant priority. I did not ask for help, nor did any fall into my life.

And *that*, is another problem:

In homes all over this country, the woman of the house has the brunt of these dirt-removal re-

sponsibilities, even if she has a full-time job out of the house! It just isn't fair.

Since this dirt comes from the activities of everyone in the household, it makes sense that all family members should participate in its prevention and removal.

Chapter 2

So, What's *My* Problem?

John Kenneth Galbraith, MS. Magazine, April 1983, page 27:

"The unpaid labor of women is one of the great unnoticed components of the standard of living . . . . The work of the average homemaker has been calculated . . not to let women know what they were worth; it was to let insurance companies know how much husbands should be paid when their wives were injured or killed."

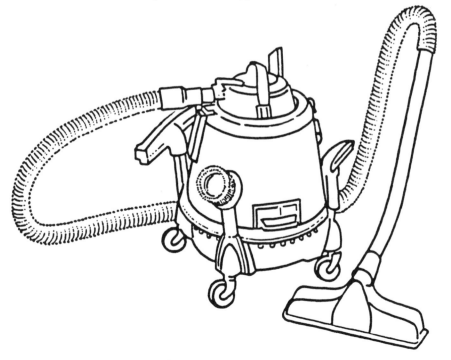

23

Note: How clean should a home be? Each family has to make its own decisions based upon how much time members are willing to spend removing the dirt! If their priority is everything spotless most of the time, then they will take the time to accomplish this feat. Those of us who want to spend as little time as possible in cleaning must set our own limits as to what dirt is "allowed" and how much we can tolerate.

Dirt (in its various guises) provides a welcome home to bacteria, and encourages safety hazards such as grease fires in the kitchen. It damages our belongings (such as causing carpets to become threadbare before their time), and is generally unpleasant and unsightly. Remember, your home is the backdrop of your life. Unless it is your main reason for living, maintain it only enough to prevent frustration. Set your goal as *low* as you can!

Chapter 2

So What's *My* Problem?

For most of my married life, I repeatedly stated that it wasn't fair for one person to have all the housekeeping responsibilities. I said this as I cleaned the toilet, washed the dishes and sorted the laundry.

In the Preview issue of Ms. Magazine, spring of 1972, I read two articles that reflected, encouraged and supported my belief. They were "The Housewife's Moment of Truth" by Jane O'Reilly, and "I Want a Wife" by Judy Syfers. (After checking my copy of this magazine, 13 years later, I found "Bravo!" scribbled on the page.) These women wrote what I felt! Their words rang true to me. I celebrated these ideas and repeated their message.

But nothing in my housekeeping life changed. I continued to take control and responsibility for most housekeeping tasks.

Nobody has ever called me patient! I am not the kind of person to allow an unhappy situation to exist. I have always confronted problems in order to find a solution. Yet in this case I was unable to even *try* to correct what I felt was an unfair situation. After you read my story, you will be able to see what unseen, subtle pressures froze my ability to take action for change. And, *Wow!* . . . if these pressures kept an impatient, confrontational person like me from taking action, what are they doing to the more patient, compliant

25

and wanting-to-please women across the country? My story is not uncommon.

When we got married in 1967, my husband Jim and I each had our own separate careers. I was an elementary school teacher; he was an architect. I remember that I had pie-in-the-sky expectations that I would be the happy homemaker *and* continue teaching.

At first, shopping, cooking, keeping house, and working outside the home as well, challenged me. The newness of our marriage, the cute little apartment, and those pretty shower and wedding gifts all helped to reinforce this fantasy. I willingly took on the shopping, cooking and cleaning responsibilities.

Jim, being a helpful sort, would pitch in when asked; and he always helped with the laundry. We would make an evening of it at the local laundromat. Later, after our first daughter was born, a vascular problem in my leg made the stairs to the washer and dryer difficult for me. He was willing and able to take on these laundry responsibilities. He knew what tasks to do and how to do them.

The novelty and newness of "playing house" soon wore off, and the onslaught of clutter began. I was overwhelmed with school work. I'd come home from school to this messy apartment, to face the task of preparing dinner in a kitchen I could barely walk through, let alone work in. After dinner, it was my job to do the dishes. Often I would opt for doing my school work (grading papers, preparing lessons, making bulletin boards) so the dishes remained a part of the great unwashed masses. If I asked Jim to do the dishes, he'd frown, but do them. I was not only feeling guilty; I was getting angry.

Meal planning and preparation gradually became a lesser priority to me. The meals I prepared were only as good as the amount of time I put into them. Hot dogs were a regular entree. The infrequent occasions when I had guests for dinner were the only times I would get the place clean *and* serve a decent meal. Talk about a double whammy! I had to clean the house *and* prepare a fancy dinner.

Why did I have all this responsibility when I was the one with more demands on my time? Even as I pondered this situation, I continued to assume most of the housekeeping responsibilities.

My problem was complicated by the fact that I was an inefficient and disorganized housekeeper. One reason that I did not push for equalizing the housekeeping tasks is because I was so disorganized. Yet, as you will see, even after I made an amazing change, I *still* had these same responsibilities.

Meanwhile, I was a teacher, and readily told everyone that my students were my top priority. Our apartment was in a constant state of disarray. And most of the mess was mine.

We had our first daughter, Jennifer. Because we felt it was important that one of us stay home with the child, and since my salary was less, I took a maternity leave. Five years later we had another daughter, Elizabeth.

27

Jenny is now 13, and with the exception of a two year return to teaching, I have not had a full-time job outside the home since her birth in 1973.

At this time, we lived in an apartment. I thought, "Now I can be the happy homemaker. Now I will cook and sew and decorate, volunteer in the community, present the family with handcrafted Christmas gifts, and even bake bread." I would do it all.

It shouldn't surprise most of you that I failed miserably. If you asked me why, I would have told you it was because we lived in a "crummy" apartment. Before I could do all those wonderful activities, I needed a house in which to do them!

When Jenny was a year and a half, we bought a house.

Now I truly would be the perfect homemaker! I was motivated. I had everything I wanted. But soon, the house was in a complete state of chaos.

My clutter had simply changed location!

I continued to have all the housekeeping responsibilities. In fairness to Jim, I must tell you that he did not come home from work and sit in front of the TV all night. He was busy with various projects and always considered parenting his top priority. He also took on the more traditional male tasks such as mowing the lawn, shoveling the snow, maintaining the car, etc.

Eventually, there came a point in time when I realized that the problem was not the location, not the messy children, not my desire to return to teaching, but *me*!

Yes, I was the cause of all this clutter. All one had to do was examine the stuff which invaded every surface, every available space, every available container, in every room of the house. Almost all of it was mine.

A few trusted friends knew what a mess we lived in; most people perceived me as very well organized. I was very active in the community and often ended up in a leadership position in the clubs and committees that I joined. I would excel at organizing a social event or a tennis tournament and get all sorts of compliments from people who had no idea of the clutter lurking behind my door. "Toni, you're so *organized!*" Hah!

People were amazed that I had so much time to play tennis! Silly people. They thought I played tennis *after* I had completed all my chores.

If these misinformed people had been permitted past my front door, they would have died! Well, actually, I would have died — of embarrassment — and occasionally did.

In 1975 two acquaintances of mine dropped by to give me their reservation for a dinner dance I had organized. I can still recall the feeling in the pit of my stomach, as I saw them approach. I knew that these two identical twins were very organized and remembered that they liked to polish silver.

Should I invite them in? There was macrame cord strung from one end of the living room to the other.

Toys were strewn about. Piles of "stuff" were scattered every which way. Of course it would be impossible to vacuum or dust such a mess. The entire scene was not only unsightly, it was *dirty*. My personal appearance was in perfect harmony with this setting. I was wearing one of Jim's tee shirts, dirty jeans, and hadn't washed my hair yet. Since I was in the middle of making pancakes I possibly had batter spattered on my face.

Deciding that they were my friends, I took the risk of letting them in. They accepted my offer of coffee and we had a nice chat. Don't ask me what we talked about. All I remember is the emotional tension I was experiencing. I was horrified because I thought *they* were horrified even though they acted as if nothing was wrong. Then to make matters worse, they even insisted on returning their coffee cups to the kitchen, which was in worse condition than the parlor!

The sad part of this story is that I truly liked them, but blocked any further development of our friendship because I decided that they could not possibly want to be my friends after seeing what a slob I could be. I didn't give them a chance.

For me to make a change, the first major step was my own realization that the problem was mine. So I began to ask trusted, organized people *what* they did, *how* they did it and *when*? I consulted with Jim's cousin, Marilyn, one of those women who truly does it all.

Marilyn has four children and an incredibly well-kept home. For 15 years she was a room mother for her

30

children's classes, an active volunteer on the PTA at both the school and district levels, an election judge, and a member of the education council at her church. During 8 of these years she was involved in Cub Scouts. She did all this while she and her husband continued to refurbish and decorate their "handyman's special". Yet she still found time for leisure activities such as gardening, antique hunting and collecting akro agate (it's a kind of glassware).

I can still remember the day she came over to help me. She told me her schedule and how she did the laundry on one day only, and did the entire job that day, including ironing and mending. And I can remember how I discarded that idea immediately. Spend an entire day in my basement? Sounded dangerous to me — I might get lost.

I did not accept one single idea from her. I wanted an organized home but I did not want to become a slave to it. Now I know, that in order to have "house perfect", somebody has to put in hours and hours each week. Since I wouldn't do that, I was continually faced with a big mess.

Years later I realized that there is a point in between the perfect home and the pig pen; that I could spend *some* of my time keeping house and thereby avoid the energy-draining mess that daily dragged me down. I also became aware of the fact that I chose to not do this work, all the while making excuses and saying I *couldn't* do the work.

In the fall of 1980, Marion Biagi, an acquaintance of

31

mine, called to tell me about a book that was helping her. I had recently dropped off a tennis trophy for her husband, without calling ahead, and was very surprised to learn that she had a clutter problem as bad as mine.

What a happy surprise! (For me — not for her!) I had assumed that Marion was one of those super-organized persons I had hoped to be. She has 8 children, always looks great, is active in the community, and had her own typesetting business. Her car was always clean, and she and her husband had just won a beautification award for the outside of their home.

"Marion!", I gleefully proclaimed, "Your house is a mess! It looks just like mine!"

It was wonderful! Newspapers, magazines, craft projects and toys were just a part of the mosaic of clutter that dominated her parlor. I knew that there were other disorganized people in the world, but I thought they all had major problems, such as mental illness or extreme poverty or quintuplets, which prevented them from being organized. Since I didn't fit into any of these categories, I figured I was unique. You can imagine my delight to find such a productive person with my identical malady!

Later I learned that Marion did not believe my exclamation that my house also was a mess. She was one of those who believed that I was extremely well-organized. And she was appalled that I would comment on her mess! Of course, I didn't just blurt it out. I thought about it first and decided that I would spare her the pain that I endured when those two sisters called on me and never mentioned the mess at all.

So a few weeks later, she called to tell me that she had been making her bed every day for the past two weeks and that this was a direct result of reading a certain book.

It is important to note that she brought this book to my attention at a time in my life when I was motivated to change. I was beginning to notice that the girls were following right along in my footsteps. It is usually charming to see preschoolers mimic adults. In this case it was not so cute. I was training them to be "slobs". I knew I had to change and was willing to try anything.

The book she recommended was *Side-Tracked Home Executives* by Peggy Jones and Pam Young. These women were writing about disorganization from a disorganized person's point of view. They wrote of their own personal disorganization, and in many instances, their stories paralleled mine. They also developed a system designed to get people like me on track.

I used the "Side-tracked" system for several months. It made a major difference in my productivity. By following their example, I learned exactly how organized people did it. This time I learned by doing. When cousin Marilyn told me her plan, I refused to try it and therefore did not learn anything from it. But, because these two sisters described my lifestyle in their book, I believed that I could improve, also.

And I *did* improve. My family and friends couldn't believe it. I worked at not allowing clutter to accumulate. I actually followed a routine to accomplish housekeeping tasks. I was able to spend time organizing closets, creating storage solutions and setting up storage systems.

What did I learn? After the elation of my success wore off, it dawned on me that I no longer had this great excuse for other family members' nonparticipation. Remember how I couldn't expect them to take responsibilities because I was such a slob? Now I could justify these expectations.

So, my problem was:

> **Even though I felt overburdened, I continued to take on all the dirt removal responsibilities, the shopping, meal planning, food preparation and after meal clean-up!**

In my gut and in my brain I knew this was not fair! Why did I allow this situation to exist? (Why do *you* allow it to exist?) The next chapter will provide some insight into this perplexing dilemma.

Chapter 3

Why are Women Chained to the Vacuum, Anyway?

A 1981 Redbook survey reported that the boring but essential tasks always seemed to fall to the wife. 80 percent of the women respondents claimed to "always clean the toilet". In 1983 the Redbook survey reported that 89 percent of the respondents were doing more than half of all the housework.

Note: How clean should a home be? Each family has to make its own decisions based upon how much time members are willing to spend removing the dirt! If their priority is everything spotless most of the time, then they will take the time to accomplish this feat. Those of us who want to spend as little time as possible in cleaning must set our own limits as to what dirt is "allowed" and how much we can tolerate.

Dirt (in its various guises) provides a welcome home to bacteria, and encourages safety hazards such as grease fires in the kitchen. It damages our belongings (such as causing carpets to become threadbare before their time), and is generally unpleasant and unsightly. Remember, your home is the backdrop of your life. Unless it is your main reason for living, maintain it only enough to prevent frustration. Set your goal as *low* as you can!

Chapter 3

Why Are Women*
Chained to the Vacuum Cleaner Anyway?

Why???... For starters, here are six reasons:

1. Most women are *trained* to do the housework. The messages we were given throughout our childhood are very much a part of us today. Because a woman is accustomed to doing these tasks, she often does not stop doing them.

2. We are accustomed to women having housekeeping responsibilities. Because family members are used to this activity, they allow and expect the woman to continue taking these responsibilities. How many people do you know who willingly add more work to their lives by taking a task from someone else? It's against human nature!

3. The woman doesn't know how to stop the cycle. Sometimes she assumes that, when necessary, other family members will voluntarily take over.

4. It is easier to do the work than it is to delegate.

---

* I know that not *all* women are chained to the vacuum cleaner. Some of us are chained to the stove, or to the dust mop, or perhaps to the laundry room. I personally rarely *touch* the washing machine. With this vacuum cleaner attached to my body I'm afraid I'll get electrocuted.

Confrontations with uncooperative family members may result in the woman deciding it is not worth the "fight".

5. Even though a woman desires that others participate, she may feel guilty that others have to do "her work", further compounding her frustration at all the tasks now confronting her.

6. It may be difficult for a woman to give up control of an area that has been her major responsibility, regardless of her hope for greater involvement of other family members.

Most of these reasons, you'll notice, stem from the dynamics of the family situation. They are a combination of the housekeeper's actions or non-actions and the family's actions or non-actions.

There are other, more subtle forces acting upon us that we probably do not realize. One such force is our economic system. There is a constant influx of new products on the market because capitalism encourages the manufacturing and distribution of goods.

We are encouraged to buy. We are made to believe we need, must have and can't live without many items which will become useless, sometimes in a matter of weeks or months. Many of these new products require *other* items for their storage or care. It is possible to find a separate cleaning product for almost everything you own, a special container in which to store it or carry it around, and finally a trash masher to more easily destroy it.

Where do we put all this stuff??? Most of mine was located on the invisible dining room table. (I knew it was there, supporting all my accumulations, but nobody could actually *see* it.)

The people who really do use their trash masher to get rid of useless products are probably clutter free. Many of us, however, have been influenced by Benjamin Franklin — "Waste not, want not" — or by the Great Depression. Being frugal and resourceful is very important to us.

We can not discard anything that someone, somewhere, at sometime might need. Of course we all believe that two days after tossing something in the garbage, our lives will depend upon this item. How many of us still have our pet rocks? I rest my case!

A relative of mine has an incredible collection of styrofoam meat trays she saves from supermarket meat packaging. When I asked why she doesn't throw them away, she told me that they make nice containers for baked goods. I tactfully did not remind her that she has one hundred and fifty ceramic plates in her china cabinet. I know it makes her happy to make use of something and it distresses her to trash a potentially useable object.

The result is that our households continue to increase in density as we add to our collections and save every conceivably usable item.

And now, the coup de grâce: *House Gorgeous.*

Not only are we stimulated to buy, buy, buy, we are indoctrinated to save, save, save. A third American ideal adds icing to this cake. It is the phenomenon of the beautifully decorated, clean-as-a-whistle, eat-off-the-shiny floor house.

We see it everywhere. Open a current magazine. I challenge you to find a lived-in household scene. Neatness thrives, almost to the degree of sterility. Where do the imaginary people who live in these fabricated structures keep their toys, magazines, papers, photos, and plastic meat trays?

I truly enjoy watching The Cosby Show, a situation comedy that is currently the most widely watched program on TV. It depicts a loving, caring family that typifies America.

What kind of home shelters this typical family? A spectacularly neat one. There is a "token" mess in the *son's* bedroom; however, the rest of the home looks like a furniture showroom. I am irritated that this show reinforces a fantasy environment; I am also irritated with the choice of depicting the son's room as a mess. This depiction reinforces the fact that it is funny when a male is a slob. When a woman can't keep her spaces orderly, it's not funny; there is something *wrong* with her.

Remember June Cleaver? She wore high heels, a dress and pearls while she dusted and vacuumed. Even Edith and Archie Bunker's house was neat.

The realization of why we have so much and why we

can't get rid of it should be helpful to those of you who are feeling the strains of this catch-22. Perhaps you would be able to get organized if you could begin to let objects go. Maybe you simply have too much stuff! Remember, the fewer possessions you have, the easier it is to get them organized.

In order to lighten our load, each of us has to redefine our needs. When I was striving for a beautifully groomed and decorated home, I failed miserably. Since I couldn't reach my goal, I got the exact opposite. Now I strive to have a home that serves the people within, not a home that enslaves me. Its function is to provide shelter and a pleasant environment for our family, storage for our possessions, and space for our activities. Its purpose is not to be an "All-American" showcase.

Our adoption of materialism and thriftiness has made the achievement of House Gorgeous very difficult to attain. However, the glue that binds women to housekeeping tasks is basically our agreement with society's traditional expectations of our domestic behavior. Somewhere along the line we chose to accept the responsibility to achieve this high ideal.

This is the key to our being able to detach some of these tasks from our workload; let's now choose to only take on *some* of these tasks.

Chapter 4

I'm Getting Off the Vacuum.

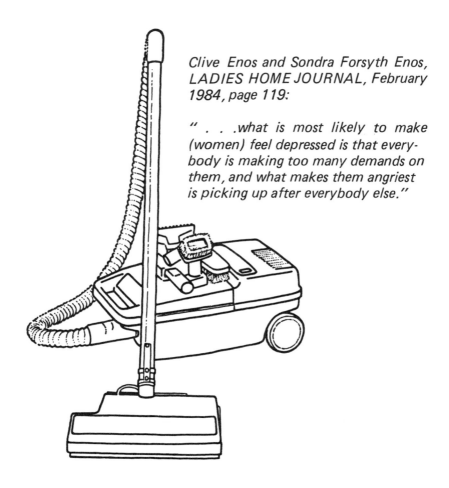

Clive Enos and Sondra Forsyth Enos, *LADIES HOME JOURNAL, February 1984, page 119:*

" . . .what is most likely to make (women) feel depressed is that everybody is making too many demands on them, and what makes them angriest is picking up after everybody else."

Note: How clean should a home be? Each family has to make its own decisions based upon how much time members are willing to spend removing the dirt! If their priority is everything spotless most of the time, then they will take the time to accomplish this feat. Those of us who want to spend as little time as possible in cleaning must set our own limits as to what dirt is "allowed" and how much we can tolerate.

Dirt (in its various guises) provides a welcome home to bacteria, and encourages safety hazards such as grease fires in the kitchen. It damages our belongings (such as causing carpets to become threadbare before their time), and is generally unpleasant and unsightly. Remember, your home is the backdrop of your life. Unless it is your main reason for living, maintain it only enough to prevent frustration. Set your goal as *low* as you can!

Chapter 4

I'm Getting Off the Vacuum!

In the process of trying to become a perfect homemaker, I learned that this is *not* how I wanted to spend my life. Once I knew how involved, how time-consuming it was to be a truly organized homemaker, I decided it was not my priority in life. However, I did not wish to go back to living from one pile to the next. There had to be a happy medium somewhere between supermom and self-fulfillment. To find this "happy medium" I have bounced from one end of housekeeping standards to the other.

What did my husband think of all this? He hated the continual mess. When he confronted me with his displeasure, I'd agree with him. I hated it too, but felt helpless to change. After I did change, a friend asked him what he thought and he said he was "stunned". This is the first time I ever heard that word cross his lips!

Did he volunteer to take on additional tasks? Not really. Before I improved, he did all the laundry and I would put the clothes away. Well, actually, I often left the clothes in the basket and dumped them somewhere when he needed the basket for another load. When I "got organized" he began to put the laundry away. Now we share this task with our children.

Today he is much more involved. In addition to the laundry, he is in charge of the entire kitchen after

45

dinner. This involves supervising the children. He frequently reorganizes the refrigerator, straightens out a messy drawer, puts away the groceries, takes out the garbage, and cleans off any dirty surface that he notices. The most wonderful part of this for me is that he does not take me for granted. He usually respects the value of my time and does not assume that his time is more important than mine. If he needs a button sewed on, he gets a needle and thread, and sews it on himself. If he needs to sew a seam on the machine, he asks me for directions.

My husband's greater participation in housekeeping tasks was a direct result of my becoming better organized. After I learned to be much a more effective homemaker, I realized that I did not want (nor was I able) to do all that we deemed necessary by myself. After several tries, I effectively communicated this realization to the whole family.

At this time our children were 5 and 10 years old. We had a very loose system for sharing tasks. I did all the cleaning, shopping and cooking. Mealtime tasks were done by other family members *if* I told them to do so. The children were to maintain their own rooms, put their clothes away, feed the dogs, and empty the dishwasher. Jim's responsibilities included laundry, from sorting to folding, all yard work, bill paying and repairing everything that broke, a regular occurrence for homeowners.

I began to notice that I had very little leisure time. I was especially irritated after dinner because everyone would leave and I would be stuck with most of the

46

clean-up — unless I remembered to delegate to the girls or ask Jim for help.

I hated to ask Jim, or anyone else, for help with household chores. (Still do!) It is rarely cheerfully given and implies a favor is being done. I wanted to be free of this *responsibility* of having to ask for help. I did not want to have to deal with it at all.

Having to ask for help actually increased my load! I had to stop and think about who knew how to do what, and who was available. Then there was the emotional burden of *asking*.

My emotions were further taxed when the response was negative, hesitant, reluctant, or whiny. When someone did come through and helped out, they were doing me a favor and that means I now "owed" them a return favor.

It was easier to do it myself.

As I was pondering what to do about this situation, Jennifer, who was 11 at the time, asked if we could have a "family meeting". She wanted more allowance! Here was a great opportunity for me to voice my concerns. So that this was not just a time to air complaints, I decided that I had to have a plan to present to the family. I wanted action, not therapy.

At this meeting, I told everyone that I felt overworked. I did not have enough time for my work, let alone time for fun. Since Jenny wanted more allowance, it made sense that she should take on more responsibili-

47

ty. This applied to Beth too, our 6 year old, who was also in favor of more allowance.

Since the "after" dinner situation was bothering me, I suggested that, after dinner, everyone take care of their own plate, silverware and placemat; and that the cook, who plans, shops and prepares the meals, should be allowed to leave the kitchen while the remaining family members tend to the after dinner chores. Before making this suggestion, I was aware that my meals left a lot to be desired. As I said before, cooking is not a high priority task with me. So I added an incentive. I promised that I would improve the quality of our dinners and that I would not leave an awful mess from food preparation for them to clean up.

This plan meant that Jim had to be the supervisor in the kitchen. It was very unlikely that he'd take on the cooking responsibilities. Would he agree to it? If so, would he follow through? Passive resistance is powerful - he could say "yes", and then just not do it.

He agreed that it was worth a try. I put more effort into preparing more appetizing meals, I did not leave terrible preparation messes, and Jim took over the kitchen clean up.

At first, he did not do everything that I deemed necessary. For example, he didn't empty the strainer in the sink. (Yuck! No one wants *that* job!) Worse than that, because he did most of the work, the girls were not learning to participate.

48

I did not immediately move in and take over. For once in my life I showed a little patience and gave them a chance to practice this job. I actually had to fight the urge to go in there and take control.

Now, almost two years later, if I don't have anything else to do, and I'm not in need of a rest, I'll pitch in. At times, meal preparation doesn't take much time or energy at all. However, I am careful to only pitch in and not get carried away; I don't want to get stuck with these responsibilities again. Besides, it's fun when everyone is in the kitchen working together.

The best part is that I do not feel that anyone is doing me a favor by cleaning the kitchen. When these responsibilities were on my shoulders, I had to *ask* for help when the load was too heavy. Now the load is shared.

Chapter 5
Give Up the Guilt!

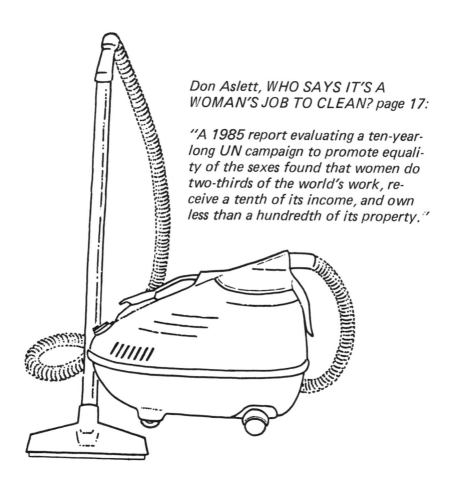

Don Aslett, WHO SAYS IT'S A
WOMAN'S JOB TO CLEAN? page 17:

"A 1985 report evaluating a ten-year-
long UN campaign to promote equali-
ty of the sexes found that women do
two-thirds of the world's work, receive a tenth of its income, and own
less than a hundredth of its property."

51

Note: How clean should a home be? Each family has to make its own decisions based upon how much time members are willing to spend removing the dirt! If their priority is everything spotless most of the time, then they will take the time to accomplish this feat. Those of us who want to spend as little time as possible in cleaning must set our own limits as to what dirt is "allowed" and how much we can tolerate.

Dirt (in its various guises) provides a welcome home to bacteria, and encourages safety hazards such as grease fires in the kitchen. It damages our belongings (such as causing carpets to become threadbare before their time), and is generally unpleasant and unsightly. Remember, your home is the backdrop of your life. Unless it is your main reason for living, maintain it only enough to prevent frustration. Set your goal as *low* as you can!

Chapter 5

Give Up the Guilt!

Are any of these scenes familiar to you?

You are angry because you feel overworked. Everyone else in the family has time to play. You don't have enough time to complete your tasks, let alone do a good job.

You feel guilty because you're angry.

You feel guilty because you are not doing a good job. (Cousin Marilyn does a good job, why don't you?)

You feel guilty because you want others to do *your work* (traditionally women's work).

You feel guilty because you know that your children are not taking enough responsibilities around the house. What are they going to do when they're on their own? You've decided that you're a failure as a parent!

You feel guilty because you want some time for yourself when there isn't enough time to do all those other things for which you're responsible.

No wonder you can't think clearly! All those emotions are stifling your ability to define the problem, consider

53

possible solutions and, finally, to take some kind of action.

Let's try to put all those emotions in another room, close the door, and take a logical approach to this situation.

It's easier to recognize the need to give up guilt than to actually give it up. Guilt-motivated actions often get some necessary task done. For example, when I feel guilty that the family is doing "my work", I can assuage this guilt by doing the work myself. This action will be accomplishing something and appear to be helpful.

When the family took over the kitchen clean-up, it wasn't as easy to leave them alone with these chores as I thought it would be. The sense of freedom was accompanied by little pangs of guilt.

What could I have done to alleviate this feeling? My first impulse was to go into the kitchen and work! But by succumbing to this guilt, I would actually be telling the family that I was *not* overworked and that their participation was *not* necessary.

I refused to give in to this negative, unproductive feeling. I fortified myself with the logic that brought us to this point and the fact that my continuing to clean up after dinner would be inconsistent with our family plan. My actions would relieve the guilt, but my resentments would continue, possibly resulting in more inconsistent behavior on my part.

The irony of acting out of guilt is that it causes *more* guilt. If I took over the after dinner clean-up, I would then feel guilty that I wasn't teaching my children to be responsible. Acting out of guilt creates a no-win situation.

I found it helpful just to know exactly what guilt is!

Guilt is the feeling caused by our inability to meet the expectations we have set for ourselves.

It also helps to know where we get these high expectations. We continue to receive messages from our parents, spouses, friends, and the media on how we "should" behave. These messages usually affect our standards by raising them to unreachable heights. When this occurs, we are at odds with ourselves. The issues in life become clouded with this feeling and the resulting behavior is not directed at accomplishing our goals but at covering up our guilt!

There is a way to determine if an action is appropriate and not guilt-motivated. Clearly define what you want to accomplish. Write it down. Talk to other family members, if it includes them. Then decide on a course of action to follow. If you find yourself feeling guilty, and you want to assuage that guilt by a certain action, ask yourself if that action is consistent with your goal. If not, then use this knowledge to permit yourself to abandon that negative action.

I am always amazed at the power guilt can have over

me. The most recent episode occurred when I brought Elizabeth to her first day of summer day camp. She had not wanted to go. I signed her up because the previous year I listened to her request for "no camp". She spent the entire summer complaining to me that she had nowhere to go, nothing to do, and no one to play with. The memory of last summer strengthened my resolve to sign her up for this summer.

So on this morning of this first day of camp, she moped around. She looked sad. Her body language matched her mopey face and pleading eyes. "You'll love it!", I said, knowing she wouldn't believe me.

She hesitated with every step of getting ready. When we arrived, she trudged into the meeting room. Our hopes that a girl friend would be there that she knew, were dashed. As I left her, her eyes said, "Please don't leave me here."

I was probably in a worse state than she. My thoughts were something like, "What have I done! What if she hates it? What kind of a mother am I anyway?"

I sat at my computer to begin my work for the day, but I couldn't stop worrying about what I *thought* I had done to Elizabeth. It was at this point that I decided to do something about this guilt.

First I had to identify the expectation of myself that I wasn't living up to. I wondered what I thought I ought to be doing. I identified a "should" that I did not wish to fulfill; it was that I ought to provide my daughter with educational and entertaining activities all

56

summer!

Immediately, I lowered my expectation. Instead of taking charge of her summer, I decided I would be very receptive to her need for quality time with me after camp. Additionally, I decided to "throw myself" into my work, and not worry about her until 2:50, the time I had to leave to pick her up at 3. I could devote that entire 10 minute time segment to worrying.

I had a very productive day.

I forgot to worry.

She loved camp.

Acting out of guilt, I might have withdrawn her registration. I might have spent the day worrying about her. Worse yet, I might have resented her for causing me this grief.

You will find the task of equalizing the workload much easier if you can get over this feeling of guilt. Remember why you feel the way you do. Recall that you have a choice when it comes to feelings and actions; that you can choose to think about something else and act according to the goals you have decided upon.

While you're working on giving up the guilt, use the same technique of choosing your thoughts and feelings, to **give up anger**. Anger is yet another unproductive emotion that only serves to complicate the issues at hand. Use your time and energies to accomplish your objectives.

Chapter 6

Equalizing the Workload

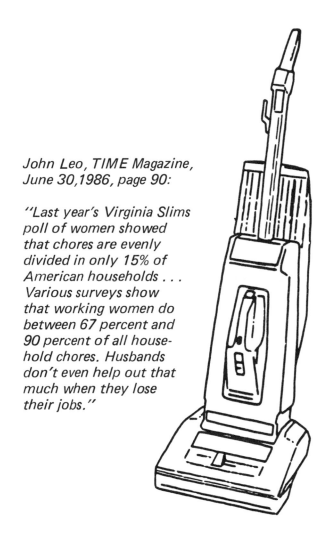

John Leo, TIME Magazine, June 30,1986, page 90:

"Last year's Virginia Slims poll of women showed that chores are evenly divided in only 15% of American households . . . Various surveys show that working women do between 67 percent and 90 percent of all household chores. Husbands don't even help out that much when they lose their jobs."

59

Note: How clean should a home be? Each family has to make its own decisions based upon how much time members are willing to spend removing the dirt! If their priority is everything spotless most of the time, then they will take the time to accomplish this feat. Those of us who want to spend as little time as possible in cleaning must set our own limits as to what dirt is "allowed" and how much we can tolerate.

Dirt (in its various guises) provides a welcome home to bacteria, and encourages safety hazards such as grease fires in the kitchen. It damages our belongings (such as causing carpets to become threadbare before their time), and is generally unpleasant and unsightly. Remember, your home is the backdrop of your life. Unless it is your main reason for living, maintain it only enough to prevent frustration. Set your goal as *low* as you can!

Chapter 6

Equalizing the Workload

This is the chapter you've been waiting for. It is the one that answers the "How can I get them to work?" question.

I have identified 10 steps which are the guidelines to follow for effective implementation of a task sharing program in your family. After the listing they are explained in greater detail, so keep reading!

1. Evaluate your own attitudes and beliefs about housekeeping issues.
2. Determine the amount of time each family member could have for housekeeping.
3. Initiate the action to get other people involved.
4. Inform family members about the necessity of sharing these responsibilities.
5. Discuss the tasks that need to be done.
6. Allow people to choose tasks in a democratic way.
7. Share your knowledge and expertise with others.
8. Agree on acceptable standards and abide by them.
9. Expect everyone in the household to contribute.
10. Don't allow yourself to slip back into old behaviors.

Some of these guidelines are easier to follow than

others, depending upon your own personality and style. However, they are all important and necessary to the fulfillment of the goal of total family participation in household tasks.

Let's examine them more closely.

1. **Evaluate your attitudes and your beliefs about housekeeping issues.** Before you begin you must agree with and understand the importance of the following statements:

   a. You've got to think positively! If you are saying, "My spouse won't do housework!", you are probably right — not because of his unwillingness, but because of *yours*. Visualize everyone in the family cheerfully sharing responsibilities.

   b. Household tasks are *not* related to gender. Anyone can learn and perform these duties. They tend to be boring, repetitive, unimaginative, and low on most people's list of desirable activities; but these attributes have no bearing on which *gender* best performs them. Give those who haven't been involved, the opportunity to learn and to be responsible for these chores. If someone refuses to do a certain chore because it is beneath their status, I have to wonder how this person values the person they *expect* to do this job?

   c. If you are a parent, it is your responsibility to teach your children to be self-sufficient. This learning process begins at home and will equip them with skills that will serve them throughout their lives. Since they too benefit from a pleasant, uncluttered home, it is only natural that they actively participate in the process that maintains it.

d. Anyone can learn housekeeping skills. The tasks are not that difficult nor complicated to prevent others from learning and practicing them. Every skill we develop requires practice. Allow them the opportunity to achieve competency. Don't fall into that "I do it because I do it best" trap.

2. **Determine the amount of time each family member could have for housekeeping.** Notice I said "could have", not "does have". This is the time to think about what is fair to each person.

The measuring stick to use is "time". Compare the amount of time each family member takes for leisure.

In "The Politics of Housework", Pat Mainardi suggests that the measuring stick to use in determining unjust situations is leisure time. Compare how much leisure time you have to the amount of leisure time other family members have. If some family members have lots of time to sit in front of the TV, or to pursue a sport or to spend in any other totally recreational, nonproductive activity from which they alone benefit, then an unjust situation exists for those with considerably less leisure

63

time. Use this logic to divert you from making excuses for your spouse or children.

You must be honest about your own use of time. While I was wallowing in disorganization I had plenty of time to play tennis. The fact is that I was unconsciously unproductive in my use of time and released this anxiety on the tennis court. I couldn't possibly expect other family members to take on the responsibilities that I continually neglected. I remember that I justified that time for tennis because it was my "therapy". This treatment did nothing to solve the problem at hand. It temporarily treated my anxiety, a symptom of my disorganization.

Now that you realize that there is no reason to expect *one person* to be solely responsible for all household tasks, and you know that sharing these duties is imperative for everyone's well-being (male & female, child & adult), you are ready to *communicate* this to the people you live with.

3. **You, yourself, must initiate the action to get other family members involved.** If you are doing most of the work, you've got the problem. They do not. As it now stands, they allow and *expect* you to continue indefinitely. If you think that they will voluntarily take over some of your responsibilities, be prepared for a disappointment. Nobody wants to admit that they are being taken for granted. Think about it. Is it possible that you

are being taken for granted and not necessarily appreciated? How do family members behave when you fall behind and the tasks are not done? Do they pat you on the back and say, "Poor Mom. You're so overworked that you didn't get my socks washed." Or do you hear, "Where are my socks? Why didn't you wash them? You *knew* I needed socks today? What am I going to *wear?*"

4. **Inform family members about the necessity of sharing tasks.** Show them a monthly work sheet (see Chapter 9). Let them see all the tasks that need to be done. They may not realize how much work is involved. Most people in a family have more interesting things to do with their time, including *you*. If it is important to you that other family members help, then you must make it important to *them*. To ease the way for them, suggest that this system be used on a trial basis — to be reorganized at a later date — not to be discarded.

5. **Discuss the tasks that need to be done.** Allowing everyone to participate in the discussion will help to give them ownership of the problem. As a family, decisions may be made as to which tasks can realistically be done. How often these tasks need doing can also be a group decision. Encourage and value everyone's input.

6. **Allow people to choose tasks in a democratic manner.** The best systems are the ones which allow for a frequent rotation of chores. If family

members are allowed a choice of many of the tasks, they will perform them more enthusiastically.

7. **Share your knowledge and expertise with others.** If you have a better system for doing laundry, teach this to the family. However, be aware that different people use different methods to complete the same task. If your spouse or child prefers a system different than yours, allow it to be done his or her way. After all the *completion of the task by someone else* is the main issue here.

8. **Agree to acceptable standards and abide by them.** So that this may occur, it is necessary to discuss the degree to which you would like these tasks completed. Perhaps you have been setting standards that are too high. Don't be afraid to compromise.

9. **Expect everyone in the household to contribute.** Old dogs can learn new tricks. If one individual is permitted to not participate, then why should *anyone* participate? One goldbrick can sabotage the whole system.

10. **Don't allow yourself to slip back into old behaviors.** If quietly and subtly the family is resisting, you may decide it is not worth the effort to continue. We often choose the old, comfortable way, even if it is frustrating, time-consuming and unjustified. Remember that change is uncomfortable. It is at these times that you need to draw on your strength and continue working towards that goal

of *full family participation*. They are waiting for you to give in. *They will test your limits*. The process of enlisting their participation may have some set-backs. Do not aid their cause! Remember, it *is* worth the effort. It is up to you to help them participate, not to help them goof off. Call another family meeting. Tell them how you feel. Discuss the behaviors, not the personalities. *Maintain a cheerful, positive attitude.* Do not call anyone a dirty, filthy, lazy pig-slob bum!

Effective communication is the key to success in getting other family members involved. Many times I have spoken to people who assumed that they communicated their needs to others when, in fact, they had only given hints.

Communication is a two way street — talking and listening. If our thought is not being received as intended, it is not being effectively communicated. And that means *no* communication! To test how well you have communicated your thought, ask the person on the receiving end of the conversation what he or she heard you say.

Remember! It is very important that your communication addresses the issues, not personalities. Do not attack anyone. Discuss the behavior that you desire. Talk about how you feel. Begin your statements with "I". "I feel . . . I'm upset . . . I'm angry . . . I'm worried". Allow them to decide how they might change their behavior. Give them time to think about your feelings.

The reason we hesitate in being direct, when we try to

communicate, is because we are not sure what the results of our honesty will be. How are our words received and understood by the listener? You must decide for yourself what the risks are and then consider if they are worth taking.

Perhaps the problems you are experiencing are more severe than the problem of uninformed family members. Discuss these problems with your family. Talk to trusted friends. Join a support group, or form a support group. Talk to an expert. Consider family therapy. Get some help!

Do what you must to solve this problem! Every day people make changes in their lives that a year ago they thought would be impossible.

Beware of *denial.* Denial is so common that we usually don't recognize it. We make excuses and frequently hear ourselves saying, "Yes, but . . ."

To illustrate our natural tendency towards denial, think about the first thing you say when you hear bad news. "Oh no! It's not true!" That statement is an automatic denial of something we do not wish to hear.

Denial is the main reason that we allow unhappy situations to exist. We keep telling ourselves that things aren't so bad. We say that we can handle it. This feeds into those great big expectations we have of ourselves. When we don't live up to these expectations, we blame ourselves and that leads to you-know-what. Guilt! (See Chapter 5.)

Be honest. Why did you buy this book? You want a change? Go for it!

Chapter 7
How Other Families Share Tasks

Art Buchwald, THE SATURDAY EVENING
POST, July/August 1986, page 14:

"I discovered . . . . that there is no such
thing as upward mobility in home
management, no chance for ad-
vancement, and no opportunity
for a wage increase."

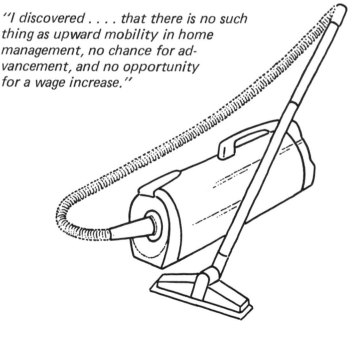

71

Note: How clean should a home be? Each family has to make its own decisions based upon how much time members are willing to spend removing the dirt! If their priority is everything spotless most of the time, then they will take the time to accomplish this feat. Those of us who want to spend as little time as possible in cleaning must set our own limits as to what dirt is "allowed" and how much we can tolerate.

Dirt (in its various guises) provides a welcome home to bacteria, and encourages safety hazards such as grease fires in the kitchen. It damages our belongings (such as causing carpets to become threadbare before their time), and is generally unpleasant and unsightly. Remember, your home is the backdrop of your life. Unless it is your main reason for living, maintain it only enough to prevent frustration. Set your goal as *low* as you can!

Chapter 7

How Other Families Share Tasks

As you've probably guessed from this chapter title, we will next see how some other families have tackled the issue of task sharing. While you are reading, be on the lookout for methods that appeal to you. Think of how you could modify these systems to solve the problems in your own unique situation.

The first system, *Lessons from Real Life: Earn Your Keep*, is the most complicated to set up. It addresses all the housekeeping tasks and involves all the members of a large family every day of the week. This system could easily be adjusted to small families. The second, *It's Economics!*, is unique in its motivational approach. The third system, *Saturday Morning Card Party*, considers many tasks, does not involve every family member of the family and is practiced only on Saturdays. The fourth, *Everyone Cooks!*, is a system that only concerns meal preparation and involves every family member. The last, *Family Quick Pick-Up*, is more of a tactic than a system and requires no planning or record keeping.

Lessons from Real Life: Earn Your Keep!

Marion and Bill Biagi have eight children, four boys and four girls. They developed this system for sharing tasks when seven of the eight were living at home. At that point their ages ranged from twenty-one to ten.

73

Marion, who had most of the housekeeping responsibilities, initiated this system. She was making some progress towards getting organized and realized the enormity of the housekeeping tasks. She decided it was time for her family to become involved.

Inspired by some systems she had read about, she asked for a family meeting. At this meeting, she announced that while the family was "helping" with certain tasks, the majority of the tasks were delegated to her and that she could no longer continue to be responsible for them. There was just too much for her to do.

Everyone in the home had a job. The school-age children had their school and homework. The adult children had their jobs. Marion had a part-time business in her home plus the responsibility for meal planning and preparation.

She presented them with a list of about 60 tasks and proposed that the jobs be divided among all family members, including her and Bill.

How could they do this? Some tasks took more time, some were particularly unpleasant, some required more skill than others. She proposed that they evaluate tasks so that it would be easier to determine individual requirements.

To begin, each member was asked to assign a value to each job on a scale of 1 to 10, 10 representing the more difficult jobs and 1 the easier jobs. (Marion admits that voting on 60 jobs in one afternoon was difficult on everyone's patience. She suggests spreading this task out over several days.)

After this evaluation, each job received an average point value. For example, five people valued dishwashing at 6 points, two gave it an 8, and two gave it a 3. It received a total vote of 54 points, which averaged out to 6 points. Dishwashing was then assigned a point value of 6 points.

The jobs were then placed in categories according to the frequency that each was to be done. Daily, every-other-day, weekly, etc. The values were then totaled for each category. Dividing the total by 9 (7 children and 2 parents) gave a new value - the score each person was to earn during that period. (Don't panic! Read on . . .)

For example, if the daily chores needing completion add up to 72 points, dividing them by 9 people would result in 8 points worth of jobs. Each family member would be responsible for earning 8 points a day in daily tasks. For weekly chores, the total was 40 points. Dividing 40 by 9 means that each person is to earn approximately 5 points a week in weekly chores done. If only daily and weekly chores were included, then the weekly total a member was to earn would be 61 points. 8 points a day times 7 days is 56 points a week for daily chores, plus 5 points for the weekly chores. $56 + 5 = 61$ points per week.

Points could be earned in any combination. Laundry was rated 7 points. Feeding the cat was rated 1 point.

If one person did the laundry 6 days and fed the cat 1 day, they would earn exactly 43 points for the week. 7 points x 6 days = 42 points. 42 points + 1 point (feeding cat) = 43 points.

Records were kept on a big chart (Figure 1). Each person's name was listed on the chart and they were to record what they did each day and how many points they received.

Each task was listed on an index card with a letter code (see Figure 2) and its value. Members were to choose the cards for the tasks they preferred to do and record their points (with the task code) on a chart upon its completion. The code is important. It tells everyone exactly what that person did to earn his or her points.

"Washing dishes" was a 6 point job with a code of "A". If Amy did the dishes, she would record "A-6" under her name. Recording "A-6" on a chart is easier than writing "Wash Dishes - 6".

In this system, daily points were top priority. A quick glance at the daily tally sheet disclosed who needed points for the day. Jobs still not done were then delegated to these "needy" family members.

People who earned more points than required each week were rewarded. Because of the wide range of ages, it would have been incredibly challenging to find equitable rewards for everyone. Since all of the children were able to do the jobs, *the children* decided on money rewards. Later, the family decided that

	DAD	MOM	ALISON	BILL
SUNDAY	A-6	B-5 F-1	G-7	C-5 F-1
MONDAY	H-3 F-1	A-6	C-5 F-1	B-5 K-2
TUESDAY	G-7	E-2 C-5	H-3	A-6
WEDNESDAY	B-5		G-7	
THURSDAY	H-3			
FRIDAY				
SATURDAY				
TOTAL				

Fig. 1

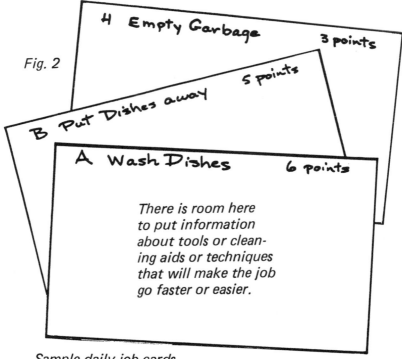

Fig. 2

H Empty Garbage — 3 points

B Put Dishes away — 5 points

A Wash Dishes — 6 points

There is room here to put information about tools or cleaning aids or techniques that will make the job go faster or easier.

Sample daily job cards

77

Fig. 3

R - Wash Kitchen Floor					12 points
1. Remove furniture			4. Rinse with clean water.		
2. Sweep. Get under furn.			5. Clean chair leg tips.		
3. Mop with deterg, in hot water.			6. Put furniture back.		
	Do by	Did job on:		Do by	Did job on:
DAD	12/9	12/7	TOM	3/17	
BOB	12/23	12/23	DAD	3/31	
AMY	1/6	1/3	BOB	4/14	
ALISON	1/20		AMY	4/28	
JIM	2/3		ALISON	5/12	
ADELE	2/17		JIM	5/26	
MOM	3/3		ADELE	6/9	

*Sample of card for less frequent chores.
Progress is noted right on the card and
moved to next person's "pocket."*

78

fines must be levied for the "slackers". Those people not meeting their quota of points were fined. These fines were used to reward those who did more than was required of them. This took the responsibility of doling out rewards, off the parent's backs. These refinements were hacked out at family meetings.

It was "scary" at first for Marion to give over the control of these responsibilities to the whole family. However, in no time the family appreciated the fairness, the flexibility and the sharing of these responsibilities. The emotional atmosphere was much more pleasant, too.

The first week was interesting. Marion and some children were motivated, positive and enthusiastic. Noticing that the older boys were not doing their share of tasks, Marion started paying close attention to every member. Bill, her husband, did not have any points recorded! Yet, he was seen working on tasks each day.

She asked for a private meeting in the family car. (Where else can parents of 8 kids get privacy?) Why, she asked, was he not recording his tasks? Well, he didn't think this system was such a good idea. She thought a minute and told him something like,

"We've tried every system imaginable in this family and none of them have worked without a lot of hassle and adult intervention. I have thought long and hard about this and it is the best system I can come up with. It has the flexibility that the family needs and the potential for really getting jobs done. If you won't cooperate, the older boys won't cooperate. If they don't cooperate the other children won't cooperate. That puts us right back to where we started — with me having all the responsibility for these tasks. And that is unacceptable to me."

Putting the ball in his court she said, "I give up. You find a better system and I'll be glad to support it."

He thought awhile and said that he couldn't think of anything. He agreed that it was important that everyone participate and he would be more cooperative.

The results were that almost everyone did cooperate. The children were now arguing about what task they *would* do, rather than which one they wouldn't. It was heaven on earth for Marion to hear the kids fighting over who gets to do what job! "Don't anyone do the dishes . . . I need the points!". . . (whiny tone), "Ma-ah-om, Bobby did the laundry and I said that *I* wanted to do laundry today!"

One adult child could not adjust to this system. There were several traumatic episodes resulting in this child's departure. At one family meeting this person asked to be excused from some of this work. A valid reason was not given. The family took a vote. Their decision was that *all* family members were required to participate or *none* would.

While this was a very difficult and painful time for Marion and Bill, it was an important lesson for them all. This unhappy adult child was unable and/or un-willing to cooperate. Marion and Bill knew they had

80

absolutely no control over this child's behavior, but they *did* have the right to say which adult family members could live in their home and eat at their table. Notice was given that people who refused to pitch in would have to find another place to live.

When this child chose to live elsewhere, it was by choice. This was little consolation to Marion. However, she knew that ultimately this was for the best. That to allow one person to not participate would be doing them more harm than good. There comes a time in parenting when you just have to let go and allow your children to live their own lives, and more importantly, to make their own mistakes. (Emotionally, this child grew a lot that year and is now on good terms with the whole family. The experience made this child stronger. Marion and Bill emphatically expressed their love to this child, while refusing to condone the uncooperative behavior.)

As time went on, Bill decided that record keeping with the more infrequent chores was clogging the system. He took all the semi-monthly, monthly, etc., task cards and divided them into 8 piles, each pile having close to the same point value. Using a pocket chart (Figure 3) with one pocket for each family member, one pile was put into each pocket. When members completed a task, they recorded the completion date on the card and passed it onto the next member.

The oldest daughter at home at the time was Alison. Jenny had moved out long before the system began. Alison is a detail person and took on the responsibility of keeping track of all members' status. She collected fines and paid rewards, and could have earned points herself for taking on this job. Instead, her parents made adjustments in her rent.

The system has had to be remodeled as the children moved out. Billy got married, Jimmy moved to Ohio, Bobby joined the Air Force, Tommy went to college and Alison found an apartment. With only Adele and Amy at home, the system has been modified again.

The benefits to this system are:

1. It's about as fair and just as any system can get. Everyone participates to approximately the same degree.

2. Since each family member is entitled to input, they have ownership of the program. In the business world, the best work is done by employees whose input is valued, sought and acted upon. This applies to the business of running a home, too.

3. This system provides choices. People may select the tasks that appeal to them.

4. It takes the delegating of tasks off the parents' shoulders thereby reducing the "bad-guy" image that parents occasionally project.

5. This system is easy to monitor. If a task needs doing, the responsibility for it falls to the person who needs the most points.

6. Its positive approach does not encourage a negative attitude. People use the system thinking, "What can I do now to get some points?" rather than "Why do I have to do this?"

7. It offers an excellent training situation for home management.

It's Economics!

Have you ever paid someone to clean your home? Would you ever consider paying your children to clean your home? Rosalind (Roz) Larsen recently heard Dr. J. Zink speak at a parent teacher meeting. This behavioral expert is the author of several books; *Champions in the Making*, (ISBN 0-942490-01-0), particularly relates to the topic of children performing household tasks.

His premise is that the children of the eighties perform better when they know how the activity will directly benefit them. So he has proposed a system whereby the selection of chores is available to anyone interested in performing them. What sparks their interest? Dollars! Tasks that are categorized as family-maintenance chores are compensated for at minimum wage.

Rosalind was intrigued with Dr. Zink's ideas. His system was totally alien to the methods she had been using on her 11 year old son, Lorin, and her 8 year old daughter, Ruth. Nevertheless, she did recognize that her methods were unproductive.

She was using the "allowance" system. Each week the children would get a certain amount of money with the expectation that they would help out around the house and keep their rooms picked up.

Here's how the allowance system *didn't* work! When Rosalind wanted some chores done around the house, she asked for help. This request was usually met with reluctance. This unwillingness generally provoked a negative response from Roz. "What do you think I am, your slave? What have you done for your allowance anyway?!!"

The children, meanwhile, immediately spent their allowance. Between paydays, they would beg for money for whatever they immediately needed. Rosalind was always amazed at their greed, at their constant demand to get this or to get that. As a child, she wasn't anything like them! She helped with chores because it was the "right thing" to do. Eventually she realized that techniques her parents used on her were not especially productive when she used them on her children.

Rosalind says she felt uncomfortable presenting Dr. Zinke's system to Lorin and Ruth, but also thought it was worth giving it a try. She began by showing them a list of household tasks. She told them that from now on, she would pay them $3.50 per hour for performing these tasks, and $2.00 per hour for babysitting. Furthermore, she informed them that they would no longer be receiving an allowance. If they were to get any money at all, they would have to earn it. They chose Wednesday as payday.

The tasks that she listed were categorized by Dr. Zink as "family-maintenance chores". The children were not to be paid for maintaining their personal belongings and spaces. As a matter of fact, they would receive their pay on payday only when their rooms were tidy.

Lorin and Ruth sat wide-eyed during Rosalind's presentation. After asking questions — Lorin explored every imaginable "what if" — they accepted the entire program! They recognized the fairness and clarity in this system, but best of all it offered them an opportunity to control the amount of money they could receive. They now would have the autonomy to make their own purchases.

At first Lorin and Ruth experimented with the system by trying different jobs. They discovered who liked to do what and learned how long each task took. Because they were being paid by the hour, in the beginning they had to record how much time each task took. Gradually, they learned that some chores always took the same amount of time. This enabled them to assign a monetary value to the task. For example, it became known that a five minute job, such as taking out the garbage, was worth thirty cents. Hence, after taking out the garbage, ".30" was recorded with a notation "took out garbage".

For this system to work, the child must have materialistic needs. During periods of contentment, there is no enthusiasm for working. However, when Lorin wants something, it is hard to keep up with his energetic demand for work! Because she is younger,

Ruth is not as interested in making money as is Lorin, but since Roz absolutely does not give either child any spending money, even Ruth has to frequently "go to work". For this system to work, it is crucial that the parent adhere to the principle of no-work, no-pay.

Another critical element is meaningful praise frequently given for specific accomplishments. Studies consistently show that productivity increases when praise is given and diminishes when praise is withheld. The best outcome for Lorin is that he not only completes household tasks, he feels his efforts are worth the trouble. He feels good about himself.

I recently stopped him one afternoon, to ask how he was doing — to ask him what was new. He told me he was on his way home to go to work. He enthusiastically said he had the best job ever — that he was being *paid* to take Ruth to the pool and that he had earned $35 that week. I was impressed with his elation over his ability to earn money. His confidence, self-esteem and attitude were obviously positive.

Rosalind is thrilled with the results. There are times when the children choose not to work; but, she reminded me, there are times when adults choose not to work. During the first week of summer vacation Lorin decided he was going to sleep late, lay around and in general, goof off. So he did. He didn't expect any pay, he didn't ask for any pay and he didn't get any pay. The next week he decided he needed something so he worked diligently.

Taking the children to the store is much more pleasant. Now, instead of having two begging, whining, demanding, crying children at her side, Rosalind is accompanied by two mathematicians. "Let's see, how many times do I have to walk the dog in order to get this water pistol?" She says that this system has lessened much of the frustration of parenting she had experienced while using the allowance method. Roz is especially impressed with the positive effects it has had on her childrens' self-esteem.

Saturday Morning Card Party

Catherine Deam has 3 children and occasionally has a foster child or two old enough to participate in housekeeping tasks. Her husband, Mac, works at least 10 hours a day, 6 days a week. His participation in household tasks is limited to putting his plate in the dishwasher and bringing his laundry up from the basement. He also does not make any messes for others to clean. The amount of leisure time he has is devoted to parenting. He coaches soccer and baseball; he spends a great deal of time with his children (and their friends).

To involve the children in the household tasks, she devised her own system using the cards she made from the Sidetracked Home Executives system. (The household tasks are all listed on 3 x 5 index cards). Each Saturday morning she takes out about 30 cards and spreads them on the counter. The children then choose 8 to 10 cards for the tasks they will complete. If someone takes a particularly distasteful job, they can get credit for two cards. After choosing cards, they immediately do the work.

This system works well for the Deams because the children "get to choose" their tasks, they all work at the same time, and the time is defined — every Saturday morning. When doesn't it work? When Catherine doesn't put out the cards!

Everyone Cooks!

When the Benton's children were 10, 12 and 14, a plan was devised to increase everyone's participation in meal planning. Since there were 5 people in the family, each member was responsible for one evening meal. *Everyone* participated. They planned it, gave a shopping list to the shopper, and were responsible for the preparation. On the 6th evening, they ate out, and on the 7th everyone had to find or prepare their own meal.

For this plan to work, one adult must coordinate. This is a lot less work than one adult planning, shopping for and preparing *every* meal. Total family participation is accomplished with the additional benefit of variety in the menu. Best of all, it is a great way for children to learn to cook.

Family Quick Pick-Up

A few years ago, Carlotta Madonia told me about a system that worked for her family of 5. Every evening after dinner, they all took a five minute walk around the house. Each member picked up any items that were misplaced and returned them to their correct location, regardless of who misplaced them. This is a good activity because everyone participates, the time commitment is both limited and defined, and it produces results.

Chapter 8

Hooray for Jobs Outside the Home!

Elizabeth Kolbert, The Chicago Trib-une, December 15, 1985. page 14:

(Quoting Susan Strasser, NEVER DONE), "The main reason that these tasks never attained the same status as work outside the house, she said, is that, 'more and more, money came to be the way things were valued.' The unpaid labor of women in the home appeared to have little worth."

Note: How clean should a home be? Each family has to make its own decisions based upon how much time members are willing to spend removing the dirt! If their priority is everything spotless most of the time, then they will take the time to accomplish this feat. Those of us who want to spend as little time as possible in cleaning must set our own limits as to what dirt is "allowed" and how much we can tolerate.

Dirt (in its various guises) provides a welcome home to bacteria, and encourages safety hazards such as grease fires in the kitchen. It damages our belongings (such as causing carpets to become threadbare before their time), and is generally unpleasant and unsightly. Remember, your home is the backdrop of your life. Unless it is your main reason for living, maintain it only enough to prevent frustration. Set your goal as *low* as you can!

Chapter 8

Hooray for Jobs Outside the Home!

Perhaps the division of labor in our homes is not balanced because we pamper the person who "works" while not even considering the person who stays at home as a "worker".

We have all heard statements like these:

My husband works so hard all day that he deserves the right to do whatever he wants at night. Besides, I don't work.

I don't expect my husband to help with housework. He's supporting us. Besides, I don't work.

Sure he watches TV all week-end. He puts in a hard work week and needs the rest. Besides, I don't work.

We must stop saying that we don't work!

Our society has a very strong work ethic. We don't value people who don't work!! And don't underestimate the power of language. When you *say* that you don't work, it *means* that you aren't to be valued!

Housekeeping, laundry, menu-planning, grocery shopping, food preparation and clean-up, sewing, budgeting, community contributions, and most importantly, child-care, is *work*, hard *work*! So why are we feeling sorry for this person who gets to go to "work"?

Let's look at some of the benefits to having a job outside the home and compare them to the job inside the home.

1. Jobs outside the home provide a change of location, a chance to get out of the house. You don't have to work, eat, sleep, and have leisure activities in the exact same place, day in and day out. No matter how awful a job is, each job has a quitting time. And if the job is that awful, it can be changed.

2. Most jobs offer an opportunity to work with other adults. Ideas and methods can be shared. There is the chance for regular, daily, built-in camaraderie. When a worker does a good job, he or she receives praise — so important for verification of self-worth. Why do you think the woman who is home all day relies so heavily on the phone? She needs that contact with other adults. It really irritates me when I hear a man complain about his wife being on the phone "all day". It was one of Jim's regular gripes.

3. The person who works outside the home gets paid! This is an obvious declaration of worth. The more the pay, the greater the worth. Additionally, statistics show that men who make the most money participate the least in household activities. I have yet to hear of a spouse receiving a salary for homemaking.

Frequently the homemaker has control of the money but this is only by consent of the spouse bringing home the paycheck. If the breadwinner decides to take control, the stay-at-home spouse may be left with nothing. No money, no control and no credit rating — no matter how careful and frugal this person is in managing the household finances!

4. Most tasks related to jobs outside the home do not continually need re-doing. When a letter is written, it is written! Sure, another letter may need writing, however it is not the *same* letter. Washing a dish is washing a dish. It is pure repetition of the same activity that occurred one meal ago - perhaps only 4 hours ago.

5. The job outside the home may present the challenge of solving a problem. It stimulates intelligence. Some homemaking activities are challenging. Most are not.

6. In most jobs, the worker has the opportunity to change something for the better. It provides for that great feeling of accomplishment.

7. Children don't continually interrupt the person who works outside the home. While everyone experiences interruptions, there are no greater, nor more frequent, interrupters than children.

8. The worker outside the home has a better chance of entirely completing a task. How many unfinished projects are there around your

house? How many in your office or work place? And if there are several in the work place, they probably have a deadline and will be completed by this predetermined time.

9. Usually, in a job outside the home, there is a regular time structure that may be relied upon. There is a beginning time and, best of all, an ending time. Coffee breaks and lunch breaks are timed to give needed relief throughout the day.

10. Jobs outside the home are more motivational. Somebody is evaluating productivity. Workers have responsibilities they must meet and must answer to someone.

The purpose of this chapter really isn't to glorify the job outside the home. It is to create an awareness of the factors that make the work in the home so difficult. I couldn't expect my husband to take housekeeping responsibilities until I understood the burdens of homemaking.

Homemaking's reputation is not prestigious. It is as though a homemaker doesn't *do* anything. The sad part is that many homemakers reinforce this reputation because they undervalue their work and hence, themselves.

People who have never had the opportunity to experience a job inside their home, may pay lip service to the difficulties a homemaker encounters. But deep down they probably feel the way I used to. I thought being home *all day* meant I'd have time enough to do *everything*! I looked forward to the release from those very responsibilities that stimulated and challenged me, and for which I was being paid! Of course, I also told myself that if I couldn't bear staying at home, I'd go back to "work".

I thought that since I was "home", I could cook and sew and decorate the apartment. I would be able to design and make everyone in the family handmade Christmas gifts. I'd have time to volunteer at church and at school, and most importantly, I'd be a good parent.

Well, parenting complicates the entire situation. Before I had children, I had no idea how time consuming this responsibility would be. I also mistakenly believed that parenting coordinated with the stay-at-home responsibilities. **We are always lumping parenting with homemaking.** The two activities actually *compete* for our time.

In terms of time management, "I'll cook and sew and clean and be here for the kids." is very little different from "I'll take off a month to build a family room and be here for the kids." We know that someone taking a month off to build a family room isn't going to get much building done if there is a two year old to watch! So why are we expected to get the cooking, cleaning, sewing, decorating, and community volunteering done while parenting one or more children? (Go back to chapters 3 and 5.)

97

The advantages to staying at home are:

1. A parent is available for taking care of the children's needs.
2. There is potential for flexibility of time scheduling.
3. A family member is available for special needs such as making hospital visits, greeting home repair workers, running errands, volunteering for community groups, etc.

These obvious benefits of staying at home for me, were in fact the most difficult to deal with. Freedom of scheduling and lack of structure was overwhelming. What to do at what time was simply not clear! Prioritizing was difficult. I frequently rated craft projects higher than housekeeping. When I felt guilty about the clutter and mess, I'd go on a cleaning binge — only to feel guilty that I wasn't paying proper attention to the kids. So I'd stop cleaning and do something with the girls. To be productive at home, one must be flexible, persistent, and capable of continually stopping and starting tasks.

Even as I "bad-mouth" staying home, I am grateful for the experience. I chose to be here for the children. My quarrel is not with that decision; if I had to do it over again, I would make the same decision, but in a different way. I'd build in time to continue my education and keep up-to-date in my career. I now realize it is unrealistic to expect perfection of myself as a homemaker, and I would insist on total family participation.

I object to the preconceived notions that people have about the stay-at-home job. I hope that this chapter gives you a new insight to the subtle burdens the homemaker endures.

Chapter 9
Housekeeping Task Lists

Elizabeth Kolbert, The Chicago Tribune, December 15, 1985, page 14:

"Scholars studying housework say that their research has yielded some startling discoveries. For example, they have found that the amount of time devoted to housework over the decades has remained surprisingly constant, despite the spread of labor-saving technologies, from indoor plumbing to electricity, from gas ovens to automobiles."

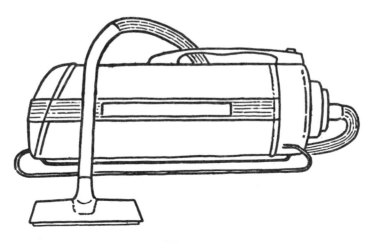

Note: How clean should a home be? Each family has to make its own decisions based upon how much time members are willing to spend removing the dirt! If their priority is everything spotless most of the time, then they will take the time to accomplish this feat. Those of us who want to spend as little time as possible in cleaning must set our own limits as to what dirt is "allowed" and how much we can tolerate.

Dirt (in its various guises) provides a welcome home to bacteria, and encourages safety hazards such as grease fires in the kitchen. It damages our belongings (such as causing carpets to become threadbare before their time), and is generally unpleasant and unsightly. Remember, your home is the backdrop of your life. Unless it is your main reason for living, maintain it only enough to prevent frustration. Set your goal as *low* as you can!

Chapter 9

TASK WORKSHEETS

The purpose of this chapter is to provide you with a listing of household tasks that are categorized by frequency - Daily, Weekly, Monthly and Less-than-Monthly. The task description is followed by the appropriate number of spaces required for one month.

You should decided how often these tasks actually need to be done in your home. If you determine that some daily tasks only need every-other-day attention, make the adjustment by only *doing* them every-other-day. I do recommend, however, that you discuss the frequency with other family members. This is a *must* if you want their participation.

I probably left out a task that you would like to include. That is what the blank lines are for. Write the task in the blank line. As time goes by, you should make adjustments to meet your specific needs.

You may want a record of *who* performed the task. The family members could write their initials in the appropriate space. Now everyone will know *who* is doing *what*!

DAILY TASKS (See grid on pages 106 and 107)

The Daily Tasks often need to be done more than twice a week. They are listed on a grid that has a space for each day of the month. The space provides a place to record the completion of the task.

For example, when the dishes are done on the third day of the month, put a mark in the box under "3" on the same horizontal as "Wash Dishes".

DAILY TASKS	1	2	3	4	5
MAKE BED					
SCOUR BATHROOM SINK					
CLEAN TOILET					
CLEAN TUB					
DEFROST SUPPER					
CLEAR KITCHEN TABLE					
CLEAN COUNTER TOP					
WASH DISHES			✓		
TIDY UP LIVING AREAS					
READ & SORT MAIL					
PUT CLOTHES AWAY					
DO LAUNDRY (as needed)					

WEEKLY TASKS (See grid on page 108)

Weekly Tasks are found on a grid with 5 spaces, a space for each week in the month. Again, use the space next to the task to record its completion, using whatever symbols your family has agreed upon. It will be easiest to consider the weeks in terms of 7 days rather than Sunday through Saturday.

"First Week" is day 1 through day 7.
"Second Week" is day 8 through day 14.
"Third Week" is day 15 through day 21
"Fourth Week" is day 22 through day 28.
"Fifth Week" is day 29 through day 31.

You may want a record of the specific day the chore was done. If Bill vacuumed the living room, dining room and den (if he has a den) on March 3rd, he would write B-3 on the horizontal for this task under "First Week". If he again vacuums these rooms on March 21st, he would write in B-21 under "Third Week". Now his family knows what he did and when he did it.

If you would prefer to do one of these tasks twice a week, put a diagonal slash mark in the space. (Someone with a dog might decide it is necessary to vacuum twice a week.)

MONTHLY AND LESS-THAN-MONTHLY TASKS

These tasks are listed on a grid with two spaces; one extra space for people who may want to do them twice a month. However, very few of these tasks need attention more than once a month. **(See page 109)**

DAILY TASKS

	1	2	3	4	5	6	7	8	9	10	11	12
MAKE BED												
SCOUR BATHROOM SINK												
CLEAN TOILET												
CLEAN TUB												
DEFROST SUPPER												
CLEAR KITCHEN TABLE												
CLEAN COUNTER TOP												
WASH DISHES												
TIDY UP LIVING AREAS												
READ & SORT MAIL												
PUT CLOTHES AWAY												
DO LAUNDRY (as needed)												

YOU decide which of these jobs need to be done daily.

106

(DAILY TASKS grid cont'd.)

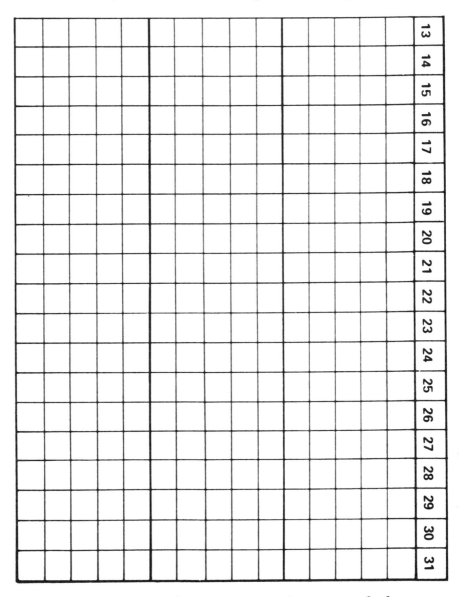

You may photocopy grids as needed.

WEEKLY TASKS	1	2	3	4	5
Plan menu for week					
Make grocery list					
Shop for groceries					
Vacuum LR, DR & Den					
Dust bedroom furniture					
Change bedding					
Empty wastebaskets					
Check refrigerator for spoiled food					
Sweep kitchen floor					
Clean bathroom floor					
Clean bathroom mirror					
Do 2 or 3 monthly tasks					

MONTHLY TASKS

	1	2
Vacuum cobwebs		
Dust under bed(s)		
Clean inside refrigerator		
Wipe outside kitchen appliances		
Thoroughly clean stove		
Wash kitchen floor		

LESS THAN MONTHLY

	1	2
Clean inside windows		
Clean picture frames & glass		
Clean ornaments in bedrooms		
Clean ornaments in LR. DR & Den		
Put drain cleaner down various drains		
Clean mirrors in LR, DR & Den		
Dust lampshades in LR, DR & Den		
Clean refrigerator grill		
Clean cannisters & knickknacks in kitchen		
Wash outside windows		

TAM ASSOCIATES, LTD.
P.O. Box 285 - S
Oak Park, IL 60303
(312) 848-6760

Toni Pighetti

Toni has spent her life wading through her own clutter. Her motivation to change came when she observed the same messy behavior in her two daughters. She knew that she couldn't help her children or expect more help from her husband until she improved herself. And improve she did!

With her partner, Marion Newport Biagi, she researched the issues of disorganization and designed a workshop to help others become better organized. Together Marion and Toni present "Conquering Disorganization" in cities from coast to coast. They continually search for systems and tools that enable disorganized people to cope and improve.

Toni is the author of the NITTY GRITTY BARE BONES METHOD OF HOUSEKEEPING CALENDAR (now in its fifth year) and THE CHILDREN'S ORGANIZER.

If you are interested in more information about helpful organizing tools and other publications, please check below and send to:

TAM ASSOCIATES, LTD.
P.O. Box 285 - S
Oak Park, IL 60303

Name . . . .

Address . . . .

City/State/Zip . . . .

I am interested in more information about:
- ☐ **THE NITTY GRITTY CALENDAR**
- ☐ **THE CHILDREN'S ORGANIZER**
- ☐ **Pad of 14 DAILY TASK SHEETS**
- ☐ **CONQUERING DISORGANIZATION WORKSHOP**
- ☐ **OTHER ORGANIZING TOOLS**

111